From Foster to Ph.D.

Dr. Danisha Keating

Dedication and Thanks

I want to dedicate this book to all foster care youth. You can do anything you put your mind to. The world is not an easy place, but there are people out there just like you. You are amazing and you can do this!

To my husband, for all of your support and love. Without you, this book would not be possible. To my siblings, I love you with everything inside of me.

A huge thank you to Michaella Mayfield for the artwork on the cover page. You brought what was in my head, into the most beautiful image. It was better than I even imaged.

Table of Contents

A Note from the Writer

Before you dig into the contents of this book, I wanted to thank you for buying this book. My hope is that by sharing my story, it will bring an awareness to the hardship that foster youth students face daily. Some foster care kids have stories like mine, and others have far worse stories of abuse, homelessness, and other hardships.

Even when people understand what foster care is, foster care kids will be asked, "So, what did you do to get yourself into foster care?" and the answer is simple... They did not do anything. Being placed in foster care is not the kid's fault but often, the kid is seen as a low life troublemaker. For the readers who may not know, foster care happens when the parent(s) are unable to take care of the child. Often, there was some sort of abuse, neglect, and/or abandonment, and the parents were deemed unfit to continue to raise the child(ren).

At the time of publication of this book, there is an estimated 424,000 kids in foster care and only 4% have graduated with some sort of college education in the United States of America. Nationally, around 2% hold a doctorate degree. The reality of these statistics should cause us to pause and ask ourselves why so many foster care kids are not finishing their degrees and find ways to help. However, many foster care kids will continue to go homeless and drop out of school.

The main reason for a low graduation rate is the lack of financial, emotional, and academic support that is needed to get through the rigor of college. Support programs for foster youth students have been created to help retain and support foster youth students who are in college. Even with these support programs, foster youth students do not know they exist because the minimal funding provided, and the lack of information provided to foster care students while in high school.

My dissertation is on Best Practice of Foster Youth Support Programs at Community Colleges in California, and a large portion of my study shows that foster youth students face homelessness, drug addiction, financial, emotional and academic hardships throughout college, and reflect the reality foster youth face.

To those of you that work with foster youth, please do not give up. You may think that you are not making a difference in that student's life, but I promise that you are. Sometimes it only takes 1 person to start believing in us. For myself, that was Susan Starr and Mr. Clark from Chaffey College.

This book contains a lot of raw emotions that have never been shared publicly before. Shame has a way of telling us that our story does not matter and that no matter how hard we fight to live, we will never truly live. Writing this book has reminded me the power of our stories and being open with others, so that they can see they are not alone. I hope that if you ever had to experience foster care, you know how loved you are. I hope to meet you and I hope that you continue fighting for your dreams. If you have never been in foster care, I hope that you are able to help love on another foster care kid whenever you get the chance.

As you read my story, you will see it has less to do with how to get through each degree program, and more about what I had to endure to get there. I hope this story can encourage you to keep pushing forward, and to push harder when things are difficult. You were made to do great things; you can do this!

I count myself one of the lucky ones.

Your friend,

Dr. Danisha Keating

Chapter 1: Dear Diary

December 2nd, 2011

Today I went to counseling for the first time and the counselor wanted to know my story. Well, I guess she wanted to know more about why I was going to counseling, and honestly, I want to deal with how I feel about my family life and how to get over it but also, I feel really embarrassed about what I've gone through. I feel alone and like the only one with a really messed up family. I know I'm not, but I mean, it's really bad. I told her I was worried about working through it all, because it's a lot and honestly, it feels like it shouldn't bug me anymore, but it does.

She told me that opening up about the past can be like trying to pull onion layers off of the onion with your hands. I guess, when you pull the layers off, it can just keep ripping into the next layer, so it's a mess. She also said that it's important to not just rip down all of the defense mechanisms that I have built up for protection, but to slowly work through these things and reminded me that it's ok to talk it out slowly and work through everything I want to.

She encouraged me to start journaling about what I am thinking but also after sessions. She wants me to also write out my family history and major events that have hurt me... I feel like that's a lot. I mean, it's pretty bad.. I'm just not sure if I should start at the abuse, or if I should start at being put in foster care or homeschooled and then thrown into school. I really dont know where to start on this but journalling seems like a good idea because writing in here is private and I can work through different things privately without getting interupted or told my feelings are stupid.... and not get lost in trying to find my words and re-read through my thought process, but also it's scary because I have to see what it is and if she wants to see it, she will see everything.

I was always told that I didn't get to have feelings. I dont know how many times I was told to stop crying or that I'm just emotional and couldn't take a joke...

Is telling someone that they are worthless and a dumb blonde, really a joke? Idk. It doesn't feel like it..

ugh! I do want to talk about what I am feeling but am I going to be seen as crazy? My emotions are all over the place, so I will need to talk it out slowly because it just feels like a lot to dig into. I mean, I know my story but it's like reliving through it again....

It's scary... I also don't want to have CPS called on me or my family again. I am done dealing with that crap.

I am going to write my story out and show her if she asks... Maybe it isn't as bad as I think it is..

Well.... Here it goes....

Chapter 2: Bruises, Belts and Empty Promises

July 20th, 2001

There are times that mom gets the belt and beats us over and over again. She yells and screams while she does it. She has even used her shoe with the heel on it and the heel bruised my back and thighs. She said if I didn't move, it wouldn't be as bad. I lost count at 19 hits.. She said she was smacking the devil out of me.

The worst part, she makes dad hit us when he gets home. He takes his belt off and then hits us a few times. Sometimes, when they hit us, the belt wraps up our back and it is not on the butt. One time, I moved, and my mom hit my stomach, and she started over and start using her fists on me. I have these bruises all on my right side of my body. I told someone about it, and they told me I was lucky. They said that if it was their mom, she would have had to grab a tree branch. My body hurts from how many times they hit us each time.

I have been hiding a secret and I don't know what to do anymore. I feel really guilty, dirty and ashamed. I feel like I am doing everything I can to run away, but he keeps finding me. When he touches me,

I know where his hands are going. I know what he is
thinking and what he is planning to do. I tried to wear
a belt, and he still figured out a way around it.

In my room, there is this short closet, but it is
deep inside. I put my bed in there, and he made me
take it out. He said I couldn't live in there, but when I
was in there, I felt like he couldn't reach me because
he was too tall and fat. I tried to hide in the attic,
where he couldn't find me. He came home from work
and said that I can't disappear like that ever again.
I've even tried to hid in the bathroom but he said that
I have to put his socks and shoes on, and then make
his breakfast but it feels like a trap.

Every day, I get up at 430am with him. He tells
me to get his clothes ironed while he takes a shower,
but sometimes, he sits on the couch and pulls me
towards him. I really hate that he sits in his
underwear. Does he do this to anyone else or just me?

I told him what we did was wrong. He said that
he wont let it happen again. I told him that we need to
tell mom and he said that he promised it would never
happen again, but it has. A lot. Not just one time or
two, but a lot. I just try to think about anything else

when I am around him and when he gets that look in his eyes, I know there is no where to run. I feel scared.

He told me today that if it happens again, we would tell mom together. I just wish my dad would not do this... this can't be what other daughters go through. When he got home from work today, he pulled me aside and asked me if I thought mom should go to a mental place... I'm only 12, why would I make that decision? I told him that he needed to be a dad and figure it out.

I don't want to be stuck with mom and I don't want to be stuck with dad. I wish I could run away. If we don't have dad, we are on the streets. Mom doesn't work. If we don't have mom, will I become his wife? Where would we go?

I wonder if mom knows what he is doing. She seems to come downstairs right when he leaves. Does she purposefully let me be a pretend wife to him so he wont touch her? Maybe that's why she hits us so hard. Maybe she is mad at him and takes it out on us... If I run away, he will go after my other sisters. If I leave, he will do this to them and I would hate that. I just wish he would see that I don't like when he does this to me.

I feel so alone and I'm so confused. I hate this... I hope nobody ever reads this. Who would believe me anyways?

Chapter 3: First Day of School

March 20th, 2004

So I finally told my mom about my dad and they told him they can't live with us anymore. The only bad thing is that CPS told us that we have to be put in school because we can't be home all day today, so we had to go to real school. Its march 13 and the school year is almost done but CPS said I had to go, so here I am. I am kindof excited becuz I have always wanted to go to school. I'm a little upset though. The counselor told me that Im 20 units behind and that I wont pass any of my classes by the time June comes. He said that he isn't going to waste his time on me and that I'm just going to fail out of school and get pregnant. Does he not know how rude he is??? He told me that if I can't get my grades to a 2.0 overall, I am going to go to the continuation school. Whatever that is….

Why are adults so rude? He sat there for an hour telling me that I should not even try to get school done and that he wasn't even going to waste his time or breath telling me what I need to do, because I was useless. What is his deal??

He was telling me that he would tell my teachers to fail me too because there is no point to me getting credits that I have to-redo anyways.... What a jerk!

He kept telling me that MY KIND just ends up pregnant and drops out of school becaz they are on drugs..... WHAT the heck?

I'll just have to figure it out on my own. Mom got to pick my eletives for me.... I asked why I couldnt pick them and they both told me "the adults are talking." WOW. OK. But I have to pass it right?? I hope I can pick my eletives next time. I really want to do cheerleading or something.

I also sat in the bathroom during lunch time because I didnt have any money for food. I was really hungry but I mean, what was I supposed to do? There are these two girls I met in PE that speak english and said I could hang out with them at lunch tomorrow. Their names are Malinda and Josie. They seem really nice and they said that what my counselor told me is stupid. They are going to help me figure out what classes I need and what I can do to get new credits.

Josie said I could take classes in the summer to catch up and redo some classes that I dont pass, and that it could help me keep on track. She told me that a contiuation school is basically where students go who dont have enough school credits in time to graduate.

I really hope I can learn things. My teacher in home ec was really mean. She asked why I didnt have the assignment done and I told her that I just got to put in the class yesterday and she said there was no excuse. I didnt even want to do this class. Well, I did but only to learn how to sow stuff but I dont want to do anything else.

OH! One of the fun classes I have is choire! I am really excited and the tacher said I have a really good voice. He wants me to try out for something called "Miller Me-Ladies" it's the all girls choir. He said that I can also try out for Chambre Singers the next time, but he already did the tryouts and did not have room for me this year.

People seem really nice but there are some teachers who are not nice.Like my pe techer seems really mean. She makes us run... alot!!!!!!! I was also told that all of next week is state testing and that we have to go into a room to do the test. I am really nervous that I wont do good. The PE teacher said that if I dont pass the state testing, I will have to retake the entire school year and Ill be hold back and repeat my first year.... jokes on her, I already have to but I HATE tests :(

I looked at all my cellabuses, these things tell you what things we have to do in class and when it is due. I'm really scared because I missed a lot and I have a quiz on Romero and Juliet in my eglish class tomorrow....... My teaher said I dont have to take it because I havent read the book yet. I told her I could try so I am not just sitting there, but she said I could help her grade some tests from last week.

I relly like that I get to go to school. I've always wanted to go, but I really hope I dont fail and I can graduate. That would be relly cool! The only downside is they dont have lockers like they do in the movies... Well,PE has lockers, but we cant use them unless we are in PE.

I have to go to bed, mom says she is dropping me off tomorrow at 5am. UGH! that is super early and class doesn't start until 7:24am!

-Me.

p.s I hope Josie and Malinda want to be my friend.

p.s.s. I hate PE.

p.s.s.s. It's really weird that I have never been to skool and I am 14!

Chapter 4 Dyslexia??

April 26th, 2004

Well I've been in school for about a month. I really like coming to school but the homework is really hard.

My eglish teacher asked to meet with me today after class, and that she would give my state test results came back and it said my reading level is at a 5th grade level and that my math is at a 3rd grade level. My eglish techer says that I read outloud very well but she thinks I have dyslexia.

She said it isn't something to worrie about because I can learn how to work with it. She said mine seems to be mild because it only hapens sometimes. She wants to work with me more because she thinks it could really help. She asked me what age I learned to read at, and I was honest with her. I was 9 years old when I started to learn to read. I told her how I would barrow audio tapes from the library with the books and read along. She said that isn't the best way to learn how to read and asked if my mom ever helped me. I let her know I was homeschooled but I wasn't really homeschooled and my mom told me that it was pointless to teach me anything because I was stupid and a girl...

I would take my sisters math tests after they were done and I would take a new sheet and try to figure it out. I also flipped to the back of the book to find the answers, so I could see how to got there. My techer said that might be why I have a hard time in math, because I never learnt right.

My techer said she would talk to my mom on ways to help me but I asked if she could just work with me because my mom doesn't really have time to work with me on stuff and I really want to leart it fast. She said that was fine. She is really concerned that my test scores will keep me from being able to graduate. She said that they are really bad and I shold be at an 8th grade level for both but being at a 3rd and 5th level means I have to do better next year on the test or else I cant walk.

It's really fruastrating that Iknow what the words are, but I dont know how the words are supposed to be on a test. She asked me to sound out the alphabet and when I got to the vowels, I couldn't do it. I felt really stupid but she said not to because everyone struggles with reading, but she really wants to help me get better so I can pass the test next year.

I relly wish mom and dad would have helped me learn when I was homeschooled, but I am really glad I will get some high school and my eglish teacher is helping me a little bit. It could help but I have alot of work to do.

I am going to go to bed, I have to be up early.

Sinercerly,

Me.

18

Chapter 5: Where am I?

October 9th, 2006

I am so upset!! CPS Showed up at school...and
we were taken away....... He said we are never going
back home!!!! WHO DOES HE THINK HE IS?????
I was at a color guard competition and got back to the
school. My friend asked me if I was ok because the
cops were looking for me last night at the football
game, but I had already left to get ready for our
competition. We were on our way back to the school
when I tried to call mom, but she wouldn't answer
which is not off for her.. She does this a lot so I asked
Kat if I could use her phone and she let me, but my
mom still wouldn't answer. When I got back to the
school, I called mom from the band room phone and it
kept going to voicemail, so I called Cilla and Jeremy.

Jeremy told me to stay in the band room
because they were trying to find me and nobody knew
where I was. He said mom was arrested and the kids
were all split up between a few homes. I told my
brother in law I was going to hide out in the guard
room, so to knock and let Mr. Sandt know he was
there. Some of my friends were telling me I could stay

at their house and one said they would bring me snacks and clothes if I hid in the guardroom.

Mr. Sandt told me that someone was at the door, but it was not my brother in law, it was CPS. They told me that I am going to Alta Loma High school and that I wont come back to AB miller. The one guy told me that I would never get to see my friends again and when I told him he was lying and that I would be back on Monday, he laughed at me. I hate when people call me sweetie… I'm not a kid… SO, I yelled at him and told him he can screw off. Who the hell does he think he is to tell me where I am going and what I am doing? He doesn't know I've been on my own. We don't need parents! We have taken care of ourselves. I don't care if I'm 15! We always taken care of ourselves!!

What makes it worse..... the CPS guy gave me a small grocery bag and told me to only grab what I needed... I was so scared.. The house was quite and felt dark. I grabed the wrong shoe, so my shoes dont match and I grabbed a shirt and skirt...

They wouldn't even let me pack anything in my backpack and said I only had 5 minutes.... Thanks for destroying my life CPS guys...

I'm just so mad. I don't know where mom or dad is and I can't even talk to my other siblings because the stupid "rule" is that I can't talk past 8pm…… DO PEOPLE STILL HAVE THAT RULE??? UGH!!! I'm with Mal and Nate in one home, my other 2 brothers are in another home, and the other three are with Priscilla and Jeremy.

Jeremy was saying something about he didn't think mom would come back... like, she's gone forever?? Bri's mom prayed with me... She told me I wasn't allowed to talk the way I did to the CPS guy because he was an adult. I mean, I get I need to respect people but he just told me I never get to see my family or friends again. When I asked when I could see my siblings he told me that it was up to what the foster parenst wanted to do and if they adopt my brothers I may never get to see them until they are adults...
WhAT THE HECK>>>????? ADOPT THEM>????
I want us to go home and I dont care what this dude says... He is such a jerk! Why would he even say those thigns????

I really want to go home. Why couldn't we have different parents?? Why couldn't they be there!!

I'm honestly scared. Ver told me that we would get out of here, but I don't know how. I feel like I have to break out of jail now! Will they arrest someone running away from home??? Or the CPS? Will the school still let me come here if I don't have a home?

I just feel so scared that we will be pushed around. There is 8 of us siblings, we wont be able to stay in the same home and they keep telling me that we "MIGHT" get to see each other... Like who the hell do these people think they are??? They just rip familys apart as if they like to do this!! I wish I was old enough to just leave here...... I don't understand why they took us and why they couldn't just leave us alone. We were doing fine. I would go home after school and do homework with the kids and get them to bed, Priscilla would pick us up and drop us off for school and when she couldn't, I would walk the kids to school and then walk to mine. I was late for 1st period a lot but my teacher knew I was coming. I mean, I know my mom would dispear for a few days but I mean, we were still fine. Mom would do her thing, and we did ours.

I don't even know who the hell these people are. The other girl that is here said that I can't keep the water on for more then 10 seconds, even if I'm washing my face and hands and teeth. WASHING YOUR FACE AND TEETH TAKE LONGER THAN 10 SECONDS!!!!!

She told me that I have to leave the light on for 15 seconds and cannot take any phone calls after 8pm. She also said that I can't be in any afterschool programs She said I have to have dinner with them every night because "we are family now." LIKE OK... YEAH YOUR MY SISTER NOW... JUST LIKE THAT... Whatever....

I really like the food but I just got here and there are so many rules. I don't know who she thinks she is to tell me what to do, I'm not staying here. We are leaving as soon as we can. She's stupid... I don't like her at all. ... "You can't do this...." And "You can't do that.." bla bla bla!!! I wonder if she would say anything if I put my fist in her face........I know I wont but I'm just so mad!!!!!!!!!!!! No wonder her parents put her in the foster home..... Ok.. that's mean... but UGHHHHHH.

I just don't get it. Who called the cops on us? Who called CPS??? I mean the electricity was on for the last week and we had some food last week. I know it isn't a lot of food, but we make it work out.

I overheard the CPS worker telling one of the band mom's that our house looked like a military dump house, the ones they explode when they are doing training? Whatever that means... He said that we boxed up a few windows with cardboard boxes and that we didn't have blankets, just bedsheets. I mean, the house does have roaches and it isn't clean but we can still survive. She asked me when I ate last and I think it was 3 days ago but I was staying with my friend's so I can go to the competiton. So I ate at their house before we left this morning.

You know what sucks even more? My birthday is in 3 days and I'm stuck here in a strangers home and all I want to do is see my siblings and be at home. Maybe they was right, maybe the kids getting taken away was my fault.... If I had just left school and focused on them, they wouldn't have been home by themselves... CPS would have never been called. This is my fault..

God, I know you don't read journals but I'm praying… if you get us out of here, I'll be a better sister and take care of my siblings. I don't want to drop out of school but I am going to do whatever it takes to get educated, so that when the day comes to take care of them, I can. Please let us go home.

I gotta go. Malachi is crying and this jerk girl is telling me to leave him alone… I can't be in the boys room… I'm going to punch her if she keeps bugging me. She isn't my mom… UGH! I want to go home.

P.S. Malachi cried himself to sleep.. He just kept saying he wants to go home too.... my heart is breaking and this hurts so much.... The other girl told me I better get comfortable.... I have to call her "sister" now! WHAT is wrong with her??? I want her to leave me alone.... I hate that I have to share a room with her.

Chapter 6: The Blue Dress

October 12th, 2006

I had to go to a meeting today. A lot has happened in the last few days. So, today I found out that CPS is going to let the 8 of us stay with Priscilla and Jeremy and we get to go with them <u>TODAY.</u> Priscilla and Jeremy have been in meetings the last few days and they were able to get approved for all 8 of us to move into their apartment!!!

Yesterday I was also able to go back to AB Miller for the first time because Priscilla took me. I talked to my techers and they are going to help me through the semester since I have to have a bunch of appointments with CPS. Patty came up to me and hugged me hard. He said that school hasn't been the same and we just cried. My friends are my family... I missed them and I was so scared I'd never see them again..

Today is my birthday, so it was extra special to see them again. Oh! I went to band practice tonight and the band and colorguard throwed a surprise birthday party for me and they all pitched in to get me this beautiful dress to wear to homecoming. They bought me homecoming tickets too so I could have a good day. My band "husband" Willy said that he missed me and he is glad I am back.. I have really great friends and I am so glad I get to be here.. the dress is the prettiest blueish green color and I love it so much. People told me that they missed me and loved me. This is the first time I ever have actually felt loved and wanted. I am so glad that I get to come back to my school and see my friends.

I still don't know what is happening with mom yet but Priscilla said that dad is fixing up the house so that the boys can stay with him. He cant have us girls because of what he did....but I am ok with that. I still don't feel safe being around him. I feel like I will be safe with Priscilla and Jeremy.

I just need to focus on getting back on track for school and staying out of trouble so they don't move me. CPS said that if I don't do everything perfectly, they can come in and put me in another home. So, I have to try to keep my grades and not start any fights, especially at the CPS guy.... The CPS guy also said that he thinks I am rude... because I yelled at him. I wish he knew he tore my family apart and all he could do was laugh at me, instead of explain to me what was happening..... I don't care if he thinks I'm rude, I told

him that he wasn't listening to me and laughed at me.
I hate him.
Mr. Sandt said that the band moms are going to help
me get to colorguard and choir practice.

I just hope I can stay with my friends and we
don't get taken away. At least at Priscilla's we will get
to eat every day. Vero was right, we broke out of jail!
I'm going to go to sleep now.

Chapter 7: Bye Bye High SCHOOL

June 10th, 2008

Well, it's official... Im a high school graduate..
During practice yesterday, Mr. counselor said, "Oh,...
you are not supposed to be here.." and I told him yes I
was and he said, "No, you didn't graduate. I forgot to
tell you that you were missing credits..." He laughed...
I fake laughed.... I rolled my eyes and walked...
He is still so rude..

I just dont get it. How are you going to work in
education and discourage students so much?
Anyways........ I GRADUATED! And I graduated
with 30 extra credits... TAKE THAT STUPID MR.
COUNSELOR!!!!

I am just trying to figure out what to do now.
Dad told me that I need to work and that school is a
waste of time. Well... a waste of time for me anyways.
He said that my dsyelxia is a sign that I should not go
to college and that the economy is crashing, so I
should just get a job and if school is something I still
want to do in a few years, then do it.
He also said he wants grand babies.. GOOOD Thing
he has 10 other kids....

I just dont get why he is so against education... He told me that women should only stay in the home because God designed us to have babies and if we disobey God, we will be punished... He said that is why I have dyselxia because God is trying to show me that I need to stay at home.... I dont understand why he twists the bible like that...

Anyways.. I think I will take a few months off and maybe start school in the spring, which would be January 2009..

I think I also want to move out.. I keep thinking dad is going to try to do something to me and I just dont want to go through that again. The way that he looks at me sometimes scares me a lot. I dont know if he would try to touch me again because I am older, but he did slap me on the butt and said it was a "spank" for touching the food... Idk... I just feel gross...

I just dont feel safe here.. And the kids broke my laptop and he said he wont replace it or let me put a lock on my door... He got really mad when I asked about it..

Idk.. I think I should move..

I'mma go to sleep now.

Chapter 8: Hello Freedom!

January 2nd, 2009

I moved out today and got my own apartment. Dad is pretty upset and said that by moving out, it means I am never allowed to come back home... He said that it was me sinning because I should only leave home if I was getting married..... Why does he push that so much??

I am honestly annoyed with him. He told me that I have always wanted to be independent and that scared him. He said that I shouldn't want to try to build anything for myself and that I should just marry a man... What is his deal?

I am really glad that I moved out but I noticed that the kids starting telling me that dad is talking mad trash on me. He told someone I was pregnant and a prostitute... What the actual hell?

The apartment is really nice. I have my own room for the first time. OH! I Am also starting school on the 15th. I have 2 night classes, and one Saturday class. One of the classes is on tuesday and one on thurday. The Saturday class starts at 8am. I really hope I do good. I am working 6am-230pm, and then class at night. It's a lot of work but I hope I can do this... I feel like I might need to quite and get a part time job. I dont know.. It's just a thought.

The money is nice though.

Well.. Over and out. I'm off to sleep.

Chapter 9: Well S*#T! It's <u>OVER</u>

May 9th, 2009

Well.... I'm freakin screwed!!! I flunked out of my first semester of college and well..... I dont know if I am going to be able to get my degree now!! How am I supposed to do this?

UGH!!! I am not going to get this. These classes are hard! So many people said college is easy and that they didn't even study for the tests... I am studying all the time and I STILL FAILED????
I need to quit my job and get a part time job. I cannot work 40 hours a week and go to school for 10 and do all the homework required. I really need to figure this out.

I talked to Alan today, he is my boss. He told me that I need to do what I need to do for school. He told me that if I go to school, I need to do great things and that I can do it. It seems like he is the only one who believes in me. As much of a brat that he can be, he can be really sweet too. I'm just glad someone is telling me that I can... I asked him what if I fail again? What if I just keep failing? He said that I would just have to try again.... UGHHHHHH I will have to figure this out. He is right.

Tonight My art teacher, Mr. Clarke said that he was misareable with his life and his wife told him that he needed to go back to school and do what he loved to do, which was stuff with art. He said something that made sense to me... HE said that we will either wake up in 10 years, happy with where we are at or we will wake up in 10 years upset that we never tried.

I want to teach college and I want to have a better life. I wont get that working in a warehouse. plus, it seems like everything I do, makes someone mad.... So, why not find something I can be good at and figure it out from there?

I want to teach...I am going to leave my job and figure this out.

It wont be easy, but it can be possible.. People make it all the time, right?

I guess there is only one way to find out...

Goodnight self.

Chapter 10: Glass Castle and Homeless

October 5th, 2010

Today we read a book called "Glass Castle" in English class. It's weird to know that someone else out there has a crazy life story too and was able to make it. So, Jeannette, the author of the story, kind of reminds me of me but different.

Her dad always promised her and her siblings this house that was so beautiful but he basically was a drunk and spent all their money and her mom was a painter. The relationship she has with her dad is kind of like the one that I had with my dad, except the sexual abuse part.... she didn't have that..

I mean, mom and dad weren't drunks but they were abusive. Dad would make me promises that he would never touch me again, but he broke that promise. I always kind of felt like my dad's mistress.. Like I was the reason mom hated me so much was because dad would look at me like that. I still don't trust him in a room alone. Mom was also abusive, but she would hit us and yell at us. There was this one time that she sat me down for 3 hours to yell at me. She told me she wished I was never born and that the day she found out she was pregnant with me, her life was over. You know what I never understood, mom and dad swear that we are blessings to other people, but they treat us like dirt at home. What's with that? Are all parents just sucky? I just don't know why mom said she prays for me to get raped and abused... She literally told me that when I was 15...

Anyways... Today's assignment was to write to Jeannette, the author, and introduce ourselves. I wonder if my professor would take an assignment like "Hey, my name is Danisha. My life sucks too... Do you want to be friends?" I know that probably isn't good enough and he wants me to go more in depth but what do you tell someone when your life just sucks, and you wish you could change every moment of it? I guess I could say something like: "Hello Jeannette,

My name is Danisha. I grew up in California my whole life and at the age of 16, I was put into foster homes. I really want to get my degree done and become somebody better. I am currently homeless and living in my car, and my parents aren't the greatest. There were some parts in your story that felt like they were mine. I bet you hear that a lot.

I know you said where your parents ended up, but did your little sister ever change her direction? Do you ever feel like you are an entirely different person from who you were as a kid or do you still feel like a kid who is just lost sometimes?

I want to change my life because poverty sucks. I haven't really told anyone but I live in my car and have been for a few months. I'm actually writing this letter from my car. I am parked outside a starbucks, so I can use the internet to work on my assignments. Honestly, I feel embarrassed by my life and I wish I had a place to call home. I wish my parents were better parents honestly. It makes me sad to know that they are still the same people and they don't see what they have done to hurt us.

Like you, I used to really admire my dad and I loved him very much but over the years, I have seen who he really is and have felt like he has broken my trust so many times. The other day, I let him know I was living in my car and I asked him if I could sleep on the coach and he said he couldn't let me live with him and take away from his children. When I asked for a blanket, he said he couldn't give to me and take away from his children….. I don't know when I stopped being his kid too... I guess that's what happens when you stop letting someone touch you... They stop protecting you?

I realize that this is probably too much information for this letter, but I feel like you'd understand and just get it. I kind of feel hopeless right now. I just don't know what to do to make my life better, but I know education is the right direction. I just feel very lonely and scared. What if this doesn't work? What if I put all this effort into getting my degree done, but I am still homeless and poor? What if I can't get a job? I really wish I could meet you.

The glass castle feels like I am reading a little bit of my story and exposing myself to the world. I know you get a lot of these letters and you are probably too busy to meet me, but I would really like to ask you some questions, like what was it like to become a writer? Do you feel accomplished? If you could give me any advice, what would that be?
I hope to hear from you, I have to go now, the streetlight went out and my computer is dying. I hate living in my car.

Sincerely,

Danisha Mayfield

Chapter 11: Some place called Home

November 5th, 2011

So, things have been interesting. Jeannette from Glass castle never wrote me back but that's ok. I have been staying with different friends, so I am not staying in my car. Last night I actually stayed with a classmate because Sara is out of town and her parents asked me not to stay there without her. His name is Carl. I met him last week when we started, but he said he has a girl roommate, so I stayed in her room. She was really nice. I have lived in over 30 different places since I turned 15 and honestly, I am just going to get a PO box, so I don't have to keep changing my address.

I really miss the feeling of home. Just being able to settle in and be in a room with all my stuff. Being homeless just kind of makes you feel loss but the last few months, I get this weird anxiety that makes me want to hop to another place. I just leave everything in boxes now and I don't unpack. There is no point in getting comfortable when people just ask you to leave, or you can't afford to stay anymore.

One of my friend's mom told me to go home to my parents, but how do you explain when your parents don't want you anymore? Well, they never wanted us.

I just want a place that you don't have to feel put together. The feeling of not walking on eggshells or worried about how your clothes look or someone looking at you funny because you want to grab a bowl of ceral instead of cooking dinner.

I want to be comfortable where I am and not asked about what I am doing and who I am hanging out with. Honestly, I just don't want to feel like people think I am a threat or dangerous to them... Just because my parents don't want me, doesn't mean I'm a bad person... I want to be in a place that feels normal. I can imagine home is the feeling of first waking up with old make up on, the feeling of being able to go to the bathroom to brush your hair and teeth first thing in the morning, but not needing to rush to do it because someone does not want you to be in the house past 7am.

Home is the secret place that you can cry and let out your frustrations without the world watching. Home is the place with the late-night tears and heartbreak that slowly heals from the safety of your apartment thin walls.

Home is where you can put your bag in the corner, take your shoes off by the front door, and fart without pretending you didn't. It's unpacking the boxes and bags and having designated places for everything. Home.... What a weird consumpt of a place to be who you are without hiding or being afraid... Home is where you get to keep your door unlocked because you are not afraid of someone sneaking into your bed.

Home is where you can relax and not feel like you moved the wrong way or are put into a conversation just to be the butt of the joke and to feel other people's judgement towards you.

Home is the smell of something baking in the oven or the fire in the fireplace. It's where you can get a glass of hot coco or a slice of bread and leave a mess behind. It smells like Christmas morning with the warmth of the fireplace going.

Home is a sacred place. A place of comfort and joy. It's a place of rest and hope. It's the place that you can dance around the room and know nobody is watching. It's not a specific place, but the place that you feel accepted and loved, without having to put up walls. It's the place that you know you can be you.

I really hope one day, I will have someplace I can call home but for now... I have to move again... this will just have to do...

44

Chapter 12: Insanity Repeating

November 24th, 2015

I am not sure exactly what is going on, but it feels like everything is being flipped upside down. Today was possibly one of the worst days of my life and I honestly don't even know how to explain it. What I do know.
Dad is in jail.

Mom is saying she can't help take the kids. I now live with 5 people in a 1 bedroom, 1 bathroom, 500 square foot apartment. There's 6 of us here and I am going to screw this up!

At least my mom recognizes that she isn't fit to take the three youngest kids, but she only offered to help financially for $100 a month. I was able to get her to write a statement that allows me to get guardianship of the kids. This allows me to enroll the kids into school, take them to doctors' appointments, and add them to my health insurance but I'm terrified. I'm 24 years old and got a call to pick up three teenagers ages 12, 14, and 16. How am I going to do this? What if I fail???

I'm going to be honest... I am pretty pissed off that we are back to square one. I can't just let the kids go to foster homes again. We went through that in 2006 and now again in 2015. At what point are my parents going to change how they act and shape up for us? At what point were they going to do better for us?

I just think it's really stupid that dad and mom couldn't be better for us. Like, how is putting us through foster care a second time, good?? I am so terrified that I am going to screw my siblings up... I mean, I am lucky they are teenagers, I just have to help them get through junior and high school... oh well, and college. I know people are saying "it's only 8 years for the youngest" but I feel like just because someone turns 18, doesn't mean they are able to take care of themselves. This is a commitment, and we are left to clean up the messes of our parents.

I just don't understand why we have to keep cleaning up their messes and people listen to them as if they are the ones being hurt. Maybe one day I'll understand what it's like to be a parent and why they couldn't figure it out... or maybe I'll mess up just like them too.

I really hope I don't screw this up and my siblings don't hate me forever. This is going to be really hard.

Chapter 13: "I love you too"

November 24th, 2015

"Dad, I love you and I forgive you."

"I love you too" ~Dad

These are the last words from our conversation... The weirdest conversation ever. It's sad that these words were only ever said when my parents wanted something, but they were never said with tender care. They were only ever abused. My dad turned himself in tonight and I am just shocked. I guess he was staying in his car and hiding out, but he turned himself in...

What now? Why does it feel like our whole world is shattered and dismantled? Why does it feel like we are so exposed to the world and every moment is being ripped apart by every police officer, CPS worker and judge? Why are people protecting my dad and vouching for him, when he lied, hurt, and abused???? WHY do people stand up for abusers like him but shame the abused????

Why do I still love my dad when he has abused me for years????? Why do I want his love? Why do I cry for him???? Why do I even care what happens to him???? Am I so sick in the head that I desire to be loved by a father who can never truly and purely love me without a sick agenda?

Am I so desperate to have my parents love me, that I am willing to put myself in continued abuse by them???

I just wish that I had better parents. I wished that someone would look at me and say, "Danisha, I love you so much and I would never ever hut you" AND their actions would show that love. Did I do something that caused them to pick me for the abuse? Did my mom tell my dad that he could "have me" and that's why she didn't protect me? Is that what love is, and I am just too stupid to see the difference between what I think love is and what love really is?

For once, I just wish that love was gentle. Pure. Happy. Every time a love song comes on, I just wish that someone would feel that way for me. I hate that love has been shown to me in this way. I wish I could experience real and pure love! UGH! I just keep repeating myself!

Chapter 14: A Poem

March 4th, 2017

Paper-thin Walls

When the paper-thin walls exposed the tears that stream down your face. When your heart is completely exposed on the floor and your hurt runs through your veins, how do you stand to fight another day? How do you get back up?

When life tears you down and tells you that you will never make it, and that you will never be someone better, when people tell you that you will be exactly like your parents, I hope you remember that you are more than what they think of you.

These paper-thin walls may expose everything about you. The hurt that you thought you could hide from the world, is on public display.

These paper-thin walls leave you naked in front of everyone you have ever met. Privacy does not exist through these paper-thin walls, when 6 people live within them, tension arises, and their words will hit below the belt.

The words, "I hate you" will forever ring in your ear.

The words, "I told you that you'd fail" will echo louder than the "I'm proud of you" statements.

The words, "Because of who your parents are will forever be who you are." Leaves your heart wounded on the floor.

The words that are thrown at you throughout the day, will echo within these paper-thin walls.

These paper-thin walls leave you exposed in a way that you never thought possible.

There is no hiding.

There is no running.

There is no space for you to be unexposed and unraveled.

Within these walls, you cannot get away from the shame of how you feel. You cannot take back the cursing at the top of your lungs, the screams that make you feel just like her. When you lose it, the whole world will see it and the world is waiting for you to realize that you will never be anything but......

These paper-thin walls are not steady or safe.

These paper-thin walls will fall, and you will be left laying on the floor.

Outside these paper-thin walls, the world is waiting for you to fail.

So, rise up. Try again. Afterall, they are just paper-thin walls.

Chapter 15: Enough is enough

October 24th, 2016

So, today I ended my bachelor's program and tomorrow I start my master's program! It's a quick turnaround but it is a really good opportunity to get my master's degree done in 1 year. I'll have to start with one class this quarter, but next quarter I can start taking 2 at a time and get done in a year!

I don't know how I am going to do this while working full time and taking care of the kids, but I know I can do it.

I just wish that my parents could be a part of my life. Honestly, you'd think it would be as easy as, "Hey! DO you want to do life with me?" but inviting them in means inviting drama, fear, hurt, pain. They would say things to completely cripple you. I don't want to be told how much God hates me, or how I'm a disappointment today, but tomorrow, I was something they wanted and love so much.

The other reality is neither of them have a reality of what is true and what isn't. I've had too many conversations with mom about her needed money. Just last night, she asked me if I had anything I could give her because she was struggling. I told her that I did not have anything and was very sorry for not being able to help. Instead of saying, "it's ok I understand!" She went off on me.

She told me I was a horrible person, that I was just like my dad, and that I should help her...... I think she forgot that I am raising her kids.... So, I reminded her.... UGH!!! Why do I engage in these fights?????? I STRAIGHT UP SAID, "All my money goes to raising your kids! I'm overdrawn in my account.... If I had extra money, I'd give it!!"

WHY DO I ENGAGE!!! It never makes the conversations better with her. It only ever makes it worse. These conversations always break me to pieces. It always ends in me being told I am a disappointment and a failure... in a couple of months, she will say she loves me and is so proud of me.... She doesn't even know who I am. We haven't had a real conversation since I was 13.

Every time we do talk, she is telling me how I am brainwashed, that I remember stories wrong, and what I remember isn't true.... And the worst part, is if I try to confront the conversation we had last time, I'm a liar.... I've even shown her screenshots of our conversations and she has told me it was fake......

UGH!!!! I know what I need to do. I need to block her. I can't keep doing this. I cannot have abusive people in my life. If I won't have an abusive friend or ex, I cannot have an abusive family member. I can't keep doing this to myself. It creates so much hurt. I'm tired of crying and hurting, I'm tired of being their punching bag....

I've blocked her on everything. I'll block dad too.... I know he is in jail, but maybe it's time to step away from people who are close to him... I just hate that I have to lose everything in order to have a normal-ish life....

Am I really losing when I choose peace over anxiety and hurt? UGH! If only I could get NEW parents who actually cared....

Chapter 16: A Victor's Letter

September 5th, 2016

Tomorrow I have to read a statement against my dad... I am not sure if I am ready. This is a letter I never thought I would get to write, let alone speak out so freely. This is my heart on a page, and I will have to look at him. The hardest part is they said he didn't admit to anything he did to me but because I reported him, I get to speak out about him. I just wish he would admit it instead of calling me a liar again.

Do you want to know what the shittiest part of all of this is? I feel like this is my fault. Like I did something to deserve this and to deserve what he did to me... Why is it when we are abused, the abuser makes us feel like this is our fault? Like I wanted it? If I was a better person, like he wouldn't have chosen me? Sometimes I feel like I deserved what happened to me... I know it isn't true, but why do I feel like this???

UGH!!! I just feel like I only will get one shot at telling him what I feel and what he has done. I never want him out...... If I ever find out he did this to someone else.... I wouldn't be able to live with myself... I don't even know what to say but I think this is the gist of what I want to say to his face... Here goes....

Hello,

My name is Danisha, I am one of the daughters of the defendant, Dan. I remember the first incident when I was about 8 or 9 years of age. It should have been in the year of 1998. I remember the first time feeling like what he did was normal, almost like it was an everyday occurrence. I believed that the way he touched me, was what other fathers did as well, until I realized that something just wasn't right. I was sitting with a friend at the park of my old church; we were talking about her dad's interaction with her. She said "My father would never do anything to make me uncomfortable..." I was nine years old at that time and I remember feeling so ashamed. Guilty. I felt like the other woman. I felt like I caused my dad to cheat on my mom. I felt I was the end to my parent's marriage. Years later, they divorced, and I was sure, my mother blamed me for what my father did to me.

I have felt many emotions during my life... especially lately. When another report came out about my father molesting someone else, I couldn't live with this… I have fallen into a huge depression and guilt that this was my fault... I swore I would never let this happen to anyone else and he swore to me that he would never touch anyone.

He told me so many times that what he did to me was a mistake, a slip of the hand, a simple misunderstanding…

When I told him at the age of eleven that if he touched me again, he had to promise he would tell my mom because I couldn't withhold this secret anymore, he said "She will be so mad. I promise you this will never happen again, but I promise if it did, we will both tell her together." There was comfort in his lies, and it continued to happen for two more years, but we never told my mom until I, alone, told her at 14 years old and he completely denied it. When I found out about what he did, I felt that him touching another girl was my doing and my fault.

I have felt many emotions over the course of 15 years. Guilt. Shame. Depression. Unworthy. Insecurities. I endured 7 years of abuse by this man, one who I considered my hero and my favorite person, someone I felt I could trust and not trust at the same time. My hero, the man I looked up to, became the man I feared. The one I couldn't be left in a room with. The one that his eyes turned black in the night when he would decide that I was no longer human enough to not hurt. The man who believed that my body was his for the taking instead of a little girl he should have protected. I was property to him. I was nothing.

To have to sum up how he destroyed me in just 5 minutes…. It doesn't do me justice. It doesn't seem doable. What he did to me and now to others has brought shame, guilt, depression, bitterness, anxiety, depression, nightmares and even attempts of suicide and self-harm.

He not only hurt the victims, but he also hurt his own child. He hurt his family. His mother. His brothers. His Sisters. His friends. His family and his community… But he has also hurt himself.

As I am trying to sum up how I feel he has affected my life, I am realizing more and more each day that I cannot put a scale up against how I feel. I never understood how much his actions have destroyed me as a person, but this last year it was clear as day. I am so afraid to get close to people because I am afraid that if I love someone the way I loved my dad, innocently and fearlessly, I will not see the destructive patterns they hold in their lives. I have pushed away every person who has ever meant anything to me. I have purposefully destroyed my relationships because I don't feel good enough to be with anyone. I told people that I don't get close to people because it scares me too much to be vulnerable...

I fear a man touching me and often have to tell myself it is ok to fall in love. I fear being left in a room alone with a man. I fear walking places by myself. I fear sleeping with the light off in my room. I fear intimacy. I fear looking at a little girl and her father and wanting what they have…I fear marrying a man like my dad. I fear having a baby girl and having someone hurt her so carelessly. I fear having a baby boy because I fear he will follow in this man's horrible footprints…. But what I fear the most…Is the fact that I believe this man shouldn't suffer for what he did.

My mind is such a mess because as I stand here, I feel like I am going to get in trouble for sharing these words, like I'm punishing him for something that I could have stopped him from doing. I fear that I will put the blame on myself for not fighting harder and sooner to stop him because now there are multiple victims…. It could have stopped with me, but it didn't. And that is something I will forever live with. What I also fear, is waking up one day and having him stand at my door to tell me that he got off the hook…. That one day my daughter will come to me and say that Grandpa touched her…. I fear the day that I will have to ask him "WHY us? What did we do wrong to be dehumanized for your moment of pleasure??? Why did you want to hurt us when we looked up to you?"

What hurts as well, is knowing that my father will never be at graduations. Weddings. Performances. Christmas's, holidays, birthday parties, births of grand children or even be able to be left in a room with a child… If my father was willing to take advantage of his own daughter, young children, his own flesh and blood- who would ever protect us?

Now, every financial strain relay on me. I sit at work and am unable to focus. My siblings and I, three of those are under the age of 18, are just simply trying to figure this all out. We are lost. Hurting. Unsure. Who can we trust now? As I contemplate what a "good" or "valid" punishment, I cannot say what will be justified for what he did. I cannot speak for the other victims, but what I can say is that I would never want to give him access to little girls again. I would never want to wake up to find that victims #10, #11, and #12 exist....

I wouldn't want to wake up one day to find him standing outside my house. But I also do not wish death or rape on him. I get sick to my stomach thinking about my father being humiliated in prison or "getting what he deserves" as so many people have told me. I cannot dehumanize him the way he did to me. I cannot laugh at his misery. I cannot rejoice or find joy in his pain. But what I can say is that he made a decision to not only do what he did, but he continuously found more ways to do what he did. He didn't care enough to not cause shame or long-lasting psychological issues for his victims, so why should I care how long he spends in there? Because he was my father. He was my hero. But he also became my worst nightmare.

I pray that his heart is right with Christ, because that is the only one who can save him. I cannot allow this man to walk around free to hurt others. I hope that you consider his sentence, not for my sake and pain, but for the victims labeled #1-#4. To the ones who haven't spoken out because they are too afraid of him. The ones he won't admit to because he is too afraid to get more time…... or feel more shame… think of us. This whole process has made me feel less. Made me feel ugly and empty. Completely dehumanized.

Yet, I still forgive you Dad. I just can't allow you to hurt anyone else. You will never understand or acknowledge the hurt that you caused.

From the daughter you should have protected,

Me.

Chapter 17: Broken & Broke

April 16th, 2017

The hardest thing in life is finding the ones you love don't trust you. That somehow because of who you came from, labels you as garbage and broken. That no matter the redemption story of your life, you are still dirt beneth their feet. I am heartbroken and broke in so many ways that I can't even think straight.

I realize more and more each day that some people will let their trust of you break on the littlest things and they seem to never find you good enough. Someone told me today that no man should ever choose me to have children with because I will end up like my mother and this person found out that my dad is in jail and said that if I am willing to do that to my parent, what would I do to them??? What does that even mean????

Haven't I been punished enough for having the life I had? Why do people think that it's ok to hold me accountable for my parents' mistakes? Why do I get blamed when they FINALLY get caught??? I feel like their mess ups are on display but I'm the one getting blamed. If they knew what my dad did, if they knew what my mom did, you'd think they would understand?

I feel like suddenly the world is ending.

Suddenly the trust is fading.

Suddenly the conversations you have behind my back are screaming in my face. That somehow, for the mistakes of my parents, I am being punished too.

Not only have I lost my relationship, but I have lost friends due to this. People just cut you out of their life when you are going through a shit show... AND to add to the heartbreak, I am financially broke! My account is overdrawn and today, my van broke down... in the freakin RAIN!!!! And the kids were in the car with me, so of course, my complete meltdown of everything happened right in front of them AND they probably think I am a total NUT!!!! I swear, I am ending up like my mom and I hate it so much!! Why can't I react normally instead of in complete outbursts of anger???

How do you keep pushing forward when life is crashing down around you? Will I always completely lose it and just go crazy, or will I ever figure out how to be calm and collected?????????

Seriously, you should have seen me lose it. I was freakin punching and I MEAN punching the steering wheel and yelling and cussing and just going nuts....... I think I even tried to kick the van at one point when I was outside.... I am such an embarrassment!!!!

After Noah and I figured out how to put the belt back on in the engine, I just got in the van, and we left. It slipped a second time, and that's when I lost it......

I just pray that my siblings don't ever think I regret taking them in. This isn't even about them. I just feel like my life has been shattered to pieces and I am trying to pick up all the glass to put it back together and I just keep getting cut.... horribly!!!

I need to go to bed.... I just feel like a failure.

Chapter 18: New chapter, Same Damn Book

May 1st, 2017

It's rare for people to talk about how they changed the direction of their toxic family. Maybe it's because it's difficult, or maybe because not a lot of people try to change it. I'm not really sure but today, I am making the decision to continue to change the direction of my family's course. I guess it starts with one of us, right? I am just so tired of going in the same direction and having the same conversations about how I wish it was different.

I may not know what I am doing but I vow as of today that I will not have toxic people in my life. I will not have people hold my past against me. I will not let people tell me that who my parents are, is who I will be. I am who I am, and I am not who they are. If that means that I am the black sheep to people who is doing things differently, so be it.

I want to be a generational CHANGER not a follower. I want to do good for the world around me and help people that I met. I want to encourage people with my story but also hear their story. I want to create room at the table for people to sit and to know we are not in competition against each other.

What I want more than anything else, is for every person that I meet, to know that they are loved and adored. To feel safe. That they matter and that they are important. I want to open my home for holidays so that nobody is left alone and sad.

I am tired of having a new chapter in the same damn book. It's time for a new book!

It's time for a new book....

Chapter 19: Pep Talk... For real

October 25th, 2017

I finished my master's program today and this is it... I am ready for my life to completely change. I feel like I am getting better at life and dealing with stress, but I feel a new direction coming on. I don't know what I'll be able to do with my master's program and I don't know what my life will look like in a year, but I hope that it isn't what it's been. I'm ready for it to be different and I am going to work hard to get there.

I am going to do a PhD program in January and get a job teaching. I want to change other people's lives and not just focus on myself. I feel really good about this and feel like there are different doors I can go in with my life. I know it will be hard, but I feel like I can do this!!!

If I have to work full time, raise kids and get through this PhD, I will do the long days and the long nights. It will be the most challenging thing I ever have done, and I am going to do this in 3 ½ years!! I am going to do what it takes to get to where I need to go!

Also, Mark is amazing. I hope we get married! I love seeing how his dad loves on his mom, and how his brother loves on his wife.. It's a different kind of love that I have always wanted. This is it!!!

LET'S GOOOOOOO

Future Dr. Danisha...... Dr. Pepper.... DR.........
Danisha......

I can do this!

Chapter 20: Letters from a Suitcase

July 30th, 2018

It is interesting how life plays out. You grow up in the same environment but each individual experiences a different reality. We have choices to make, every day, that will determine the course of our future. We live a life that is delicate, but often taken for granted. Life is short, it is fragile, and the broken road is easily mistaken as the only road we can take.

Today I found out that one of my family members did something wrong. How can two individuals who grew up in the same environment, choose two entirely different route? When you know the way, you grew up sucked but choose to still go down that route? We experienced the same things, our reality of our everyday life was the same, expect I was older. How did this family member simply give up? Simply not care about actions. What thoughts were they going through or experiencing? What is going on in their heart?

It is crazy to me to think that we are prone to walk in the foots of our parents, even when they are wrong, but are we really prone or is it a choice we make? Did we really make the choice willingly or have we lost hope?

Honestly, I am confused. I am confused on how someone who used to be so gentle, was ok with his actions. The last 3 years have been an embarrassment to my family. I just don't know how one allows their heart to get so far away from God and so far away from church. The hardening of the heart is not a fast thing, but one that happens every time. We learn this in the Bible with Cain and Abel, with Pharaoh and Moses, even with Adam and Eve.
I guess that's it… We make a choice to do something that we shouldn't, because we allow our hurt to run the course of our lives…

Selfish ambition takes over the heart and leaves the person paralyzed, but thankfully not too far away from God's heart if they desire to change.
Honestly, my heart hurt... I am confused to why they took the route they did. I know it causes embarrassment and a sadness when I share my story. but did they ever think that what they did was embarrassing? Or is it just that I am sharing my side?

It hurts sometimes to think they walked so far away from the course without thinking of the consequences. Sometimes I want to know what they were thinking and why they did what they did, but I never want to try to understand them because I wouldn't want to expose my heart to that understanding. I cannot judge them, but I do pray for them. I know that God will use this for his glory if they allow God to change their hearts truly and deeply, but the consequences are theirs to endure. This is not something they can blame on others, they have to accept this in their own hearts, that doesn't sit with me well at all.

I think what I have a harder time, is that I value family and I desire to feel that somehow, we all came out normal after the years of abuse. We all endured so much under the hands of my parents, and I wish I could say we all made it through and were strengthened by our relationships with just the siblings, but I feel like somewhere along the way, we all just got left behind in some way or another. It hurts my heart to know that we all were hurt so deeply and never knew how each sibling felt and we all found ways to cope with it...

I would never understand the feeling of wanting to numb the pain or to cope with feeling in control... Mine was education. Although education helps me in the long run, I became addicted to show that I could do it. I could finish what I started and become better than who I was or what I was set up for, what I forgot was to enjoy the process, to understand that the world didn't fall on my shoulders to fix and that it was ok to slow down and simply process my emotions.

I hope I have gotten better at recognizing what I feel and where I am heading, but I need to realize the process is the process. My hope for myself, is that I do not give up or fall to my knees when tragedy happens.

How does one process tragedy correctly? Slowly. Very slowly.

Chapter 21: It's Ok not to be OK.

December 19, 2019

Something that I am learning more and more each day is that it is ok to not be ok. It's ok that Christmas time feels sucky and that holidays are filled with sadness. It's ok to miss people and to cry about it. It's also ok to be mad at people who chose to be destructive. It's also ok for us to feel what we feel and to know that it could have and should have been different.

It's ok to feel so broken that you just cry it out. It's ok to realize that you just needed to be loved largely... It's ok to be depressed and angry, anxious and sad. It's ok to have big emotions and to feel all of the things that you feel. It's also ok to not feel anything at all.

What is not ok, is to consistently tell yourself that you have to hold it together and to be all the things for everyone. It's not ok to push yourself to the limits of self-destruction and isolation. It's not ok to feel alone and unloved.

Self, it's ok to not be ok with any of the things you have gone through. It's ok to figure it out at 15, 24 and 30. HECK! It's even ok to figure it out at 50

and 60. Whatever you are trying to figure out and
work through, it's ok.

It's ok to not be ok and to still try to process
everything you feel and think.
It's ok to tell people when they have hurt you.
It's ok to protect yourself and set boundaries.
It's ok to tell yourself that this person doesn't get that
same access to your heart.
It's ok to put up safety barriers so that others don't
destroy you with their words.

It's going to be ok and the world may not stop for
you, but you are allowed to stop for yourself, put your
hand on your heart and say, "it's ok to be broken and
to be healing at the same time."

Chapter 22: Dear Mr. Counselor

June 29th, 2021

Dear Mr. Counselor,

This is the letter I wish I sent to you, but never could get the courage to. This letter has taken me almost 17 years to even write on paper. You do not even remember my name or who I am, but I remember yours.

When I first came to the school, you told me, "I'm not wasting my time with you. You will not graduate. You will end up at the continuation school. You'll get pregnant and drop out of high school, so don't even ask about Universities…I'd be surprised if you even stayed here next year because of your grades."

Some people might say your words were meant to encourage me and to push me to greatness, and that I should use your words as a flame to my journey, but I've been meaning to tell you something really important. I have carefully looked for the right words for 17 years.

So, here they are……

Your words were the most discouraging words I have ever heard. They were the words that beat my mind down into depression.

They were the words that pushed me into addiction. It was the words that made me cry in the bathroom stall in high school when I failed my math exam. Your words kept me up at night when I failed out of my first semester of college. Your "tough love" beat across my heart as I slept in my car when I was homeless. Your words were the words that whispered, "you'll never get there. You are nothing."

For some people, your words might have been their "motivation," but for me, they were my nightmare. They were the words that repeated my parents' words. They were the words that repeated by abusive ex boyfriend's words. They were the words that I would repeat to myself over and over again as I looked at myself in the mirror, "you are a failure. You are nothing. No matter how hard you try, nobody will see you. You are just a statistic." They were the words that kept me on the ground and pushed my self-esteem down. They were the words that crippled me for so long.

The last time I saw you, it was my high school graduation practice and you jokingly said, "Oh you are not supposed to be here… You were failing" I played it off and said back to you, "Yeah, but I did make it, and that wasn't because of you." We laughed, but inside, I cried. I hated what you had told me because it made me feel like the only thing, I deserved was trash.

But Mr. Counselor, I want to tell you something. Today I defended my dissertation for my PhD program that I finished in 3 years, 5 months, and 11 days. This is statistically rare. For the last 17 years, your words held a weight of defeat over my mind, my heart, and my being. Your words told me I could not. Your words reminded me that failure was around every turn, no matter how hard I tried to overcome it.

The sad reality is, I know your words were not "wise" or true, but they were words that YOU genuinely believed over my life. You honestly believed that I could not and would not be anything more than a statistic. What I wished for more than anything was for one person to believe in me, and you decided that day that it was more important to remind me that I was just a statistic, and I was not a human being. You used your words to tear down a 14-year-old girl who just needed one person to breathe life into her mind and heart, so she could breathe life back into her dreams.

All I ever wished for, was for you to believe in me on the first day that I met you. Heck! I wish you believed in me the last day I saw you, but what I hope you see is that your words hold so much weight. I do not want an apology from you, but what I do wish is that the next student you sit down with, you choose your words carefully. Believe in the student who does not believe in themself. Forget the statistic of who may or may not fail and pick up the words of encouragement.

Look past the knowledge that you know and breathe life back into a heart that has been beat down into defeat. Please remember that you are able to change the world, don't blow your chance because of the "pattern of students' that walk through the door." You might think that your "tough love" words fuel the fire to the student's desire to try harder, but I hope you understand that the words you say send people over the edge. You are in a position of power, do not abuse it. Do better.

Sincerely,

Dr. Keating

a student you didn't even try to believe in.

Chapter 23: Dear Mom and Dad

September 10th, 2021

Dear mom and dad,

I swore this would be the letter I would never be written and every time I have tried to write it, my mind goes blank. I think we are all at the age that we realize that our words can fall on deaf ears and that we don't know what we don't know.

Honestly, I've tried to write this same letter over and over again, and I feel like I always cross it out or it comes off too hateful or spiteful...... Funny that's how being abused works. Even writing it in a journal, you are afraid to say how you feel or felt. Chances are you either have to break into my home to get this journal or somehow, it's sent to you... There's so much anxiety and ripped up pages that goes into writing a letter to both of you.

I have always felt ashamed of being able to say the truth and how I feel. Shame in putting myself first and protection myself from your words and actions. I'm starting to realize that broken people, break people but that doesn't give them a reason to continue to break those around them.

I've been past the point of trying to understand why you both allowed the abuse and manipulation, but also why does it keep continuing to happen? Honestly, all I want to say is this, I wish you happiness and I wish that your life is exactly the way that you imagined it would turn out.

I do not hate you, but I have come to realize that I am way stronger now because of everything I went through. I do not thank you for allowing it, but I am glad that I was able to overcome it all.
I honestly don't even know why I am writing this, but I guess I felt I needed to.

I know that I have accomplished a lot in my life, I was able to overcome poverty, homelessness, raising my siblings, and getting my degrees completed. Someone asked me if I ever wished that you both were there for these moments, and my honest answer is, I stopped wishing for that a long time ago and now I just try to strive to do better for myself.

There was a long period of time that I wished you were there, but I grew to realize it was only going to be hurtful, but I realized, I wasn't wishing for the parents you were, I was praying for the parents I wish you could have been. I think there is peace realizing that who you were and whom I became are not tied together. I do not hold your faults against you, and honestly, I don't hate either of you. I honestly have no feelings towards you and just hope that as your life goes on, you find happiness in whom you have become.

I am really proud of whom I became and whom I grew into. So, I guess that is it... That's my thoughts and I'm pretty sure it didn't make any sense at all.

Dr. ME.

P.S. I know this is petty, but it would be funny to have them refer to me as Dr. instead of daughter LOL. Good thing nobody will ever see this! LOLLL

DR. DANISHA OUT!

Chapter 24: Dear You

October 1st, 2021

Dear you,

I am really glad you were able to read this letter and I hope that it can bring you some encouragement. The world can be a really cruel place and the people who are supposed to love us and protect us, are often the people who hurt us the worst and the most. For that, I am so sorry.

I wish I could meet you and just hug you. You deserve to be loved and cared for, and I am so sorry for whatever you have had to endure.

If I could give you any "wisdom," I would say don't give up. I know the road has been hard, and there are things that you have gone through that have torn you apart. I also know that there may be some things that you have never told anyone and that you feel ashamed about.

I know that there are people out there that have said that you are not worth it, or that you are dirty, or they picked someone over you, but I want you to hold on. You are worth being loved and known. You are also worth investing in. The world may be cruel, but we have the opportunity to love those around us, be a light in the dark world and to be someone who can speak truth into someone's heart. Sometimes the only thing we can do is sit with a friend who is going through a hard time and show them that we are not leaving.

So, as you prepare to go out into the world, I want you to remember a few things. I want you to look at yourself in the mirror and tell yourself you are worth it. Go on! I know it might feel silly, but sometimes we are the only voice telling ourselves that we can do it.

When the world tells you to sit down, stand up. When they tell you that you are not worth the time or energy, find people who will encourage you to try! When someone tells you that you are not worthy to be loved, find the people who tell you that you are loved. When the world tells you that you are stupid for investing in your dreams, let their words run in one ear and out the other.

Hurt people will always hurt other people but we have the opportunity to stay far away from those people. We have the opportunity to make things happen. They may not be handed to us; we will have to work hard to make it happen but I promise you that you will be happy you tried.

And lastly, the world will try to take you out, but you only get one shot at this, so just try your best. One of my first college professors said, "You will either wake up in 10 years happy with the decisions you have made, or you will wake up pissed that you didn't even try. So, you do the hard work now, or you end up doing it later. Choose what you want to wake up to."

So, friend, what will it be? Will you wake up happy that you got back up or will you spend the next 10 years wishing that you tried again?

Yours truly.

-Me.

Chapter 25: Graduation Day

October 14th, 2021

I honestly never thought I would get to this point. It's graduation day and I get to walk across the stage. I mean, I know I dreamed of it and pretended that I'd get here but to actually be here, feels insane. I don't know how many times I sat in my car pretending that I was in a room full of people telling them my story or giving a graduation speech as a valedictorian. I never got the chance at being a valedictorian, but this feels even better!

This moment also feels really tainted because I just keep thinking, "if only my parents would have been different.... they could have been here... They should have been here..." I don't know why but every huge milestone will always be met with that feeling. I think what gets me is that they COULD have done better, and they chose not to. I know some people will say, "they did the best they knew how to" but honestly, I think every day we have the choice to stay where we are or to change what we are doing. They had a choice daily, and they decided to stay in what they knew. I'm not bitter towards them and I do not hate them, I just don't understand how you can bring children into the world and not take care of them...

I need to stop thinking about that but at the same time... I'm scared of whatever is next. I've worked really hard to get here, but what if I don't make it? What if all this work keeps me living paycheck to paycheck? I know I won't follow in my family's footsteps, but I wish I could rub off on them.

I'm really hoping I can go somewhere and be somebody. Maybe I can give speeches at graduations to encourage people... I could see myself doing that but at the same time, what wisdom do I have to give? Who knows really? I mean, I look back on my life and know it is crazy to realize how far I have come. From living in poverty, walking to get to high school, and living in my car, to being able to walk across the stage to celebrate becoming a doctor. In all honesty, it does not feel like my life.

I do not feel like the same person that I was 15 years ago, or even a year ago. I've changed so much but, I know that I am not where I want to be either.

There's this pressure from people to have it all figured out and to have every moment planned. It's debilitating honestly. I keep having these moments of complete panic and awe. The panic is, what if all this work doesn't bring anything good?

I mean, I guess that is something that happens to everyone, but why are we not talking about this? We don't need to have every moment planned out, right? Can we celebrate the wins and rest? Honestly, I am not sure what to do next.

I know that I want to teach, I mean, that has been the entire point of all of this, but I am just really proud of myself for not giving up.

There were a lot of times that I could have, and honestly, I don't know what kept me going when I could have stopped, but I am really glad I kept going. Several people have encouraged me to write a book about what it was like going from foster homes to getting a phd. I dont think they really care about the degree itself, but more about how I made it. I mean, the crazy thing is that only 4% of the nation has a doctorate degree, but only 10% of foster youth have graduated with a degree at all. So, I think they want to know more about what I went through and how I still pushed forward. I pushed forward to show other people that we can do it.

I finally feel like I am at a point of my life that I am not having to start over, I am just starting new. I guess it's time for a new book.

Signed,

Dr. D

Chapter 1.0: New book, new chapters

Today

It's interesting how we work so hard to arrive at a particular point in our life, and somehow, we are still surprised when we arrive there. We doubt ourselves every step of the way.

Do you ever wonder about the exact moment you stopped believing in yourself? Do you remember that moment? I think I was 5 years old. I wanted to be a medical doctor and because my mom said I sucked at math, I stopped believing in myself. Regardless of all the negativity I have felt, or for the million times I doubted myself, I am glad I never gave up.

I do have to say, I am glad that I have lived every horrible moment in my life, not that I would wish to live through it again, but I am glad I can relate to others. I hope that when someone tells me their story, I do not dismiss it but offer grace. Offer a listening ear. Offer compassion.

Today, I embark on my journey as a professor. I have imagined this moment for 12.5 years, and to be honest, I never thought I'd actually reach this point, but I am so glad that I stuck it through. I am so glad I am here!!

I keep thinking of the days of sleeping in my car. Struggling just to get a passing grade. Struggling to figure life out and still, I dont understand the weight of having a PHD. I do know the weight of finally being in a place that I've wanted.

Can I be honest? I'm scared… What if I hate teaching? What if students hate me? What if I lose it all because I wasn't good enough? What if, what if I am actually good at it??

I know I shouldn't think like that but MAN these doubts just flow so naturally... but I know I can either accept where I am at, and fight like hell to be good at it, or I can let fear cripple me.

I choose simply showing up and giving my best. Fear will come but I will not let it destroy me. For the first time in my entire life, I finally feel like I can breathe. I am so damn proud of myself. I am proud of pushing through the obstacles, but I am really proud that I chose to simply show up and fight for what I wanted when others told me I wouldn't be able to.

I am so proud of the person I have become, and I can't wait to see what this new year holds. There's this saying by Erin Hanson,

"There is freedom waiting for you, On the breezes of the sky, and you ask, "What if I fall?" Oh, but my darling, what if you fly?"

(Put your name here),

What if you FLY? Step into freedom boldly.

Sincerely, your friend,

Professor Dr. Keating....

P.s. That has a nice ring to it.